TURBULENCE

AND TRANQUILITY IN TRAINS

MADHU MEHROTRA

Published by True Sign Publishing House

Address: G-3, HDB Arcade, Door Sanchar Nagar, Gulmohar,
Near UCO Bank, Bhopal, Madhya Pradesh - 462039
E-mail: truesignbooks@gmail.com
Website: www.truesign.in

Turbulence And Tranquility In Trains

Author: Madhu Mehrotra

First Edition: 2025

Dedicated to those for
Whom Train Travel
is a Dream
The Journey awaited
to be Fulfilled

CONTENTS

1

Roorkee Railway Rendezvous

I was visiting the Queen of Hills, after a number of years, to attend the bi- centenary year of this hill station. Naturally curious to know its past, to know about the people who built the city, who spent time here, I roamed the lanes, by-lanes, the streets and roads. Who were the men and women who left the lands of their birth to come here?

Not an easy task as the records are not accessible to laymen like me. Picking up snippets, reading articles in the local newspapers, I became aware of names like Young, Faulkner, Everest, Allen, Cautley, Jacob, Bennett. Each more steeped in mystery than the last. Reading about each one leaves one wanting to know more.

An advertisement in the Queen of Hills 200, official, caught my attention.

Join in for a fun filled evening, if Quizzing holds your heart.

Venue : Ashok Terraces
Time : 2:00 pm
Date : October 15, 2023
Host : Hareesh Panuli & Amitra Cha
Contact : Toll free number 1800 180 4321

"Vow, if nothing else, I will get to meet the famous resident writer of this town." I thought to myself.

Touching the mobile keyboard, I rang the number.

After two tries, with

'Dialling',

'Out of range' automated messages, a recorded voice gave the instructions for registration.

"Press 1 for inquiry, Press 2 for registration."

"पूछ ताछ के लिए १ दबाएँ।

नाम दर्ज करने के लिए २ दबाएँ।"

I pressed one.

"Do you want to ask the question in Hindi or English? Press 1 for English, Press 2 for Hindi."

"अंग्रेज़ी में प्रश्न के लिए १ दबाएँ, हिंदी में प्रश्न के लिए २ दबाएँ।"

I pressed 2.

"अपना प्रश्न धीरे धीरे रिकॉर्ड करें।"

"प्रश्नोतरी में प्रतिभाग का शुल्क कितना है ?"

"शून्य, निशुल्क, निश्चिंत रहें। १ दबा कर फोन नंबर दर्ज करें। एक घंटे में आप से संपर्क करेंगे।"

Pressed 1, Duty done.

The registration was completed a short while later.

***

Having brushed up the information, I reached the venue on the given day. A few participants, and many more to cheer them on, occupied the cushioned chairs, under the peach and white canopy, decorated with flowers, wall designs in wool and upturned colourful, applique parasols. A display of pan India crafts

Taking my participation badge, number 12, I sat down.

"Please feel at home, all very easy. Fun time, *chai* coffee on the house, pay for a plate of *pakoras*, two *ladoos* for every correct answer."

Some one clapped from the audience. A round of applause for the host was in order.

Puffed up the young quiz master introduced

"My co-host, Amitra, from the House of erstwhile Princely State of Samba and I, Hareesh, from the Royal House of Gaulla."

More cheering and clapping continued as the chairs were occupied

"The questions and the contestant will be picked at random from these bowls." He said pointing to the glass, fish bowls with the folded yellow and pink paper slips.

"One incorrect answer, the participant is out. A new question to the next picked participant.

If the answer is accepted the name slip goes back into the bowl. A new question to the next picked participant."

A groan went up.

"At least three tries, *yaar.*"

"We could modify, if everyone is knocked out." smiled the obliging host.

"The quiz master's decision is final. In case of controversy, the quiz master can request the participant to answer another question."

Someone waved a red flag "How many questions?"

"As many as can be answered in one hour." the host responded bravely.

"Please settle down, do appreciate a good answer. Do avoid loud interruptions and screaming answers out of turn. Let's keep it simple and joyful."

A round of applause, to show agreement and appreciation simultaneously, as the participants guffawed to display bravado and hide their nervousness.

"Ready?"

"Yeeee" cheered the crowd.

"Participant 9, Question 7......"

"Correct. *Ladoos*, please."

An attendee offered the plate to the winner.

"Question 31, Participant 19..."

"Oops, sorry, mismatch."

"Participant 20, Question 17......"

"Regrets, no, well tried.. Thanks for joining."

I began to wonder if my number was missing from the bowl.

A few more questions went past.

"Question 16, Who was responsible for the construction of the Ganga Canal? Contestant 12."

The participant next to me shook my elbow

"Yours.. answer."

"Aaa... aa" a

The jolly host repeated the question "Who was responsible for the construction of the Ganga Canal? Hint: Lived and married in the Queen of Hills; Contestant 12."

"Lord Dalhousie, 1853, I...think..y" I rattled like a brainless mugpot, rising to run towards the *'laddoo'* plate. To my mind, Dalhousie and, 1853, fitted many questions.

"Good try. But not so. It was Col. Proby Cautley, a genius of sorts."

Out of the competition, I began to do a little research on the man, who was responsible for my knock-out.

An article published in the Times of Garhwal gave some insight

"Here in the autumn of 1838, the All Saints' Church saw Frances Bacon marry Capt. Proby Cautley, who would go on to build the Ganga Canal. The couple's first home is marked as Cautley's Cottage on an old map. Later images show it as Dumbarnie; the estate now houses a school."

Further, it revealed that through his untiring effort, working for the EWD He had designed and executed the Solani Aqueduct, an engineering marvel. The Locomotive ran the Railway to transport construction materials for the canal, in 1851. It was operated by the Bengal Sappers. A steam engine, Jenny Lind, bearing the name of the famous Swiss Opera singer was shipped to India.

Wondering to which port did it come, Bombay, Surat, Diamond Harbour or Madras? How was it transported from the port to Roorkee? I found no accurate answers. To quench my curiosity, I was left to my own wild ideas and imagination. Men and animals, pulling, pushing, dragging a steam boiler. The newly trained engineers at Thompson Engineering College, now renamed IIT(R) perhaps, assembled a locomotive engine, looked for lost parts, getting the ironsmiths to remake a similar nut and bolt. The Indian juggad in operation.

The locomotive was renamed as Thompson to honour the L G of UP o O A. The locomotive moved on rails between Roorkee and Peeran Kaaliyaa, a distance of little over 6 miles or 10 km. It was meant to carry the bricks and soil to construct the aqueduct. It worked well for a few weeks before the boiler burst, due to a mishap, rendering it unrepairable.

It was discarded, the wheels removed and used for drawing animal carts.

This happened two years before the first passenger train ran between Bori Bunder and Thana in 1853.

Curious if this was the first locomotive, I probed a little more. The first freight lines were laid down in Madras in 1837. A wooden replica of what the locomotive is thought to have looked like is exhibited at Roorkee Railway Station.

So much for my attempt at quizzing, in a little hill station that lost its railway dream as vehicles with sturdy engines wind their way up and down by the thousands, causing traffic jams and temporary parking lots along the roads.

Not one to give up, I pursued the stories of railways, presenting a few to engage the readers on a train.

(The earth too is a train which we board and leave at
different stations, meeting strangers who turn into family
and friends along the way.)

2

 # Bori Bunder to Tannah 

Mrs Amelia Falkner, sat at her writing table. Ah! What a day, Saturday had been.

"Exquisitely, exotic, ecstatic!!!"

She could hear the whistle, from the Bori Bunder Railway Station.

She picked up the nib, dipped in pitch black ink and began to write to Queen Victoria. A letter of thanks was in order. A letter of informative detail was in order. No doubt, Viscount Falkner would write to the beloved monarch, but her very own Amelia should also take the trouble to give a first hand account of a pioneering journey. The journey of the locomotive from Bori Bunder to Tannah, as important as the arrival of the Royal subjects of HH Elizabeth I in Surat, the skirmish at Plassea and Booxur.

Choosing a pale white hand made sheet, Amelia wrote in her best hand

"Your Excellency, Our Majesty, Honoured Queen,

May Your Reign grow and expand, as we progress under Your Guiding Hand.

It is my privilege and delight to pen the minutest details of the events of Saturday, 16 April, in the twentieth year of Your Reign.

Your Majesty, the efforts of Your Royal servants, Your loyal Officers and native slaves has borne fruit.

With much joy, Your Obedient Maid, pens the details of the 21 mile long journey.

The station was decorated in banners, the colours of the flag of St. George, our patron saint, made a picture so pretty. An artist of high reputation perhaps can paint the image for You.

400 invites were offered and none was found missing. The invited ladies dressed in their very best, almost the Christmas dresses, dantiest of hats, walked carefully, on the red matting, softer than Persian carpets, carrying their beloved pets. Sadly, the 'No Pets' policy made them return the darlings to the maids-in-waiting. Disappointment filled their attractive eyes.

Your Obedient Maid, left for the station at the dot of two, as it is not her nature to keep others waiting for her.

Stepping into the First Class Coach, reserved for Your Obedient Maid, at 2:25 sharp, signalling that the invitees could board too. The ladies followed to take their places in the fourteen carriages. The Gentlemen and attending natives took the remaining places, according to their station in life, First, Second and Third Class.

A beautiful white screen prevented the dusty, western breeze from blowing over the three beautiful, freshly painted and polished steam engines, Sindh, Sultan and Saheb.

The Royal Guns at Fort St George were set for a 21 gun salute, one for each mile. The salute began at 3:30 and five minutes later the carriages moved, pulled by the force of steam. A gentle breeze carried the salted scent of the sea. Before it could be absorbed,

Jeannette, the maid-in-waiting, for Lady Lillian Garle, screamed, as she was not prepared for the jolt.

"Stop! Stop, let me disembark." Calming down her rattled nerves took a good five minutes. Silly girl! a lack of proper education, upsets these burdens of humanity.

Any amount of explaining that a locomotive will stop at the designated station was like water off a duck's back.

Ignoring her cries, the ladies Oohed and Ahhed at the sight of the city, going past.

Through sheer fright, she kept her eyes closed, hands folded and she prayed harder than ever before. Repeating the Rosary, she swayed from side to side swearing in between that she would never set foot on a train again.

The threat that her services would be terminated, finally set her outbursts to rest.

Thousands of people lined the tracks, bowing, kneeling in awe, trying to climb trees and balconies to see the magic, beyond their wildest imagination. Sadly, the horses running alongside raised a cloud of dust enough to make a mountain.

Caught in the delight of the moment, Yours Obediently, waved a gloved hand, only to realize how inappropriate the action was.

The first stop was at BYEEKULLA, a little rest for the exhausted engines. The crowd on the platform pushing, jostling to touch a carriage. The signal went down, the whistle blew, the carriage felt the drag, thankfully, the threat kept Jeannette calm. The trees and huts were running backwards, till a gust of soot filled steam obscured the sight.

The Sun was spinning along with the poles and pillars running backwards.

Mrs. Rott, the other lady in the cabin, turned hysterical as the clickety-clicking sound of the wheels and tracks became faster and faster.

A signal and sign board in white and red went past, reading SION.

This train slowed, the mechanics, in their fresh naval dungarees, greased the wheels, filled the boilers with water.

As it was a public holiday, more and more people were coming out, waving, cheering, raising a toast to the health of Your Majesty, Our Beloved Monarch.

As the signal went down for the journey ahead, the swaying soothed the passengers into a soft sleep, the lullaby was the even sound.

The train was now passing through the forested area, past the spires of the Church of the Holy Mother, to enter Station BAANDOOP, an upcoming suburb of the lovely city. The creek, with the fisherfolk became visible. They dropped their fishing nets to see the carriages go past. Strangely, this was the reason for less fish in the market yesterday and many families missing the fish for their Sunday lunch. It is not a complaint but the matter needs attention if this remains so, it will become a massive problem for the fisheaters.

Out of Bhandup, we arrived at 5:05 at Station TANNAH.

The band of the Indian Peninsular Railways, played the grandest tune 'God Save... .n' followed by an all time favourite 'More the..r'.

Once the natives, followed by the Gentlemen, Your Royal Maids, stepped on to the carpet. The Sun no longer visible, hidden behind the white curtain in the west, gave enough light to see the tiffin laid out on tables covered in the finest of laces.

The excitement was evident in the voices, shrill, high pitched voices conversing with hoarse loud ones, praising the journey in unison.

"Cheers, cheers, great cheers, a toast on Our Beloved Queen. Cheers, cheers, hearty cheers." resounded in the cool, now dustless air.

We went out to sit in our horse carriages, popularly known as VICTORIA as the train carriage and engines had to be attended to.

That night we could barely dance in the Club or sleep through the night. Even at Church yesterday, the conversation was overshadowed by this marvel.

Writing these words, the fingers shiver, with the very thought of the marvellous journey.

Praise to Your Majesty, Honourable Queen. May Your Reign Promote Prosperity and Progress.

May the Reign extend from shore to shore.

Your Obedient Maid

Amelia Faukner

of BoriBunder

East Indies.

3

Rats on a Train

Born in a train carriage, trains are my home. Musaak Mum, lived in the squishy squashy hole between the rail tracks. The ear shattering sounds and shaking earth were her very breath. She would take a lift, no need of permission, on the lowered wires and water pipes below the carriage, ever so often. Just for a visit to Grandma Nana Musak or climb into a grain carriage.

A few months ago, she found herself wriggling on the floor of a passenger carriage with tens of dozens of feet moving slowly, swiftly in all directions.

Scared that she would be crushed, she scampered to the far end of the coach.

"Ouch, aeee, ouch, see, see" screamed a roly poly passenger in a fine, satin suit of green, with pink flowers embroidered on the neckline.

"What's the matter? Don't scream. Sit on your berth." her companion instructed.

"A mouse, I saw a mouse, get it out, I won't be able to sleep. Ouch, it may bite my Bitwa. Ooo, cchh. "

The carriage moved, someone pushed a heavy tin trunk below the berth.

"Over" thought Mumma, closing her beady eyes as the trunk corner pricked her tail.

The floor was bouncing, rattling as the passengers tried to settle.

"Oo, these humans, always rushing around, never thinking of us creatures on the floor."

Clickety, clickety, click. Clickety, clickety, click, ran the wheels of the train.

The carriage stopped moving causing the trunk to push outwards, giving space to Mumma Musak. Breathing a sigh of relief, she scrambled towards a dazzling light that shone at a far end. Straight towards the light, she almost flew on to the over crowded platform, people, carts, luggage vans, food stalls, porters, rumbling wagons and a maze of pattering feet. Scrambling over the sacks, down a water pipe into a rushing gush of black water with bits of plastic, jute pieces and left over food.

"I am drowning" when a piece of wood came in her clutches "Swim, Missy Musak, swim" she kicked her hind legs, keeping her snout over the water level.

"Aah" she choked "uggh, ugh" the whiskers drooped, the water carried her for a few feet, bringing her to a mound of garbage, choking the drain.

"Out, out" she thought and clawed over the sticky, gluey, mound, shivering into an opening through the broken brick wall. A shrub was growing outwards.

"Ah!" as she found her way to the hollow made with the twigs.

"Who are you, Madam?" questioned Papa Musak, who was already dozing in the nest. "You are stinking, how did you arrive here?"

Missy Musak lay flat, drying her wet, sticky skin, curling her tail around her head.

"Intruder, speak or leave." said Papa Musak.

"Hmmm" Missy Musak fainted.

Hours later, she was still in the nest, where she heard the trains run

"Clickety, click, clickety, click."

"Will you be my wife?"

"I will, yes I do."

Holding their paws and rubbing their noses they went in search of food, climbing on to a grain coach. The whiskers twitched ceaselessly, below the beady red eyes.

"Vow, lovely, tasty, sweet, really sweet."

The couple ate and ate. The carriage moved and moved. At times they saw the Sun, at other times stars and a silver plate becoming thin then large and round.

"Like us, from thin to fat." laughed Papa Musak.

The burly container sack was opened and the grain poured out. The couple were pulled out as the grain rolled out. More grain covered them, gasping they pushed with all their strength to cross the floor and on to another coach.

It was full of parcels. Chewing on the jute cloth, they cut it into fine pieces, collecting it to make a warm nest. Missy was on way to become Mumma Musak, a beautiful one, settled in the warmth, giving birth to half a dozen, pink, hairless babies.

"So pretty, once their eyes open, they will be like me, adventurous, facing the tribulations."

"Chewwin, cheewin, they will be bold brats like me, living in tranquility, quietly in the corner of a train carriage or below the bench."

Our journey of life began on a train and ever since we are enjoying free rides. Better a rat on a train than below it.

4

Elephants at a Railway Crossing

Rukhesh looked at his mobile, the time, 7:42. In three minutes, the College 'local' would leave Sherpuri station and come to the Bijall Crossing in seventeen minutes.

"I have seven minutes to go across, otherwise, I will have to wait for twenty or more minutes before the barrier will rise to let the traffic go.

Rukhesh picked the tiffin carrier, placed it on the bicycle carrier and pedalled as fast as he could.

"Oh, Rukhesh, listen" he heard Anjini call as he pedalled past her on the dusty path.

He stopped the bicycle, got off and waited for her to catch up.

"What's the hurry? Let's bunk the first period or the whole day. Let's go and see the Pacific Mall." she said, rolling her bicycle.

"Bunk, I mean you talk bunk. You can, you got this cycle free, you have to pay no fee, Doctor Saab pays for your stationery and what does it matter? whether you study or not."

"Rukhesh, not fair, part of what you say is right, but we have to study."

The crossing barrier gates were down, now they would have to wait for the next twenty minutes.

"Why can't they just construct a narrow overhead bridge for bus pedestrians and cyclists, these cars can wait and speed up later" mumbled an irritated, frustrated man restrained by the lowered gates.

"Exactly, agreed his companion, all we need is a long armed JCB to pick us over.

A vendor with blue and green soft candy wool was trying to draw the attention of the children in the waiting cars. His competitor "Chane, masaale chaane, chatkaare chaane" was winding his way between the car and waiting human bodies.

A bus and a lorry halted with a screech, as the train became visible at a distance.

"Go fast, let the gates open, we are already behind schedule" Anjini said aloud.

The train was approaching at a rapid speed, when a herd of elephants began to amble across the tracks.

"Shoo, shoo"

"Huuush, huuush,..hhhaaat"

"Go, go, go back" yelled the onlookers.

Totally oblivious to the approaching train and the crowd, the herd, consisting of three cows, a bull and six calves kept moving across the track.

"Accident, accident for sure, I hope the train won't get derailed"

"Think of the animals, they are dead for sure."

The train was barely a hundred and fifty meters away from the leading animal on the track. The vegetable woman vendor threw down her ware basket, tugged a swishy, thorny branch ducked below the gate and ran to the track. Her sari caught between her legs.

"Majoli, what are you doing?"

"You want to die? Just sit down on the side."

The words did not reach her ears, as the clanging was loud enough to drown human speech.

"Swish, swish" swept the thorny branch in Majoli's hand. She moved her arms like an expert buffalo driver to speed up the sauntering animals.

"Hush, hush…. hrrrr… hush" a woman uncontrolled she swung the branches. The animals caught unaware, moved out of the track, a little faster. The engine ran past, the driver and passengers in the non-AC coaches waved at the crowd on their side of the gate.

The carriages maintained the speed. The red signal kept shining, till the tail of the train was lost.

Majoli sat on the other side, pulling the thorns out of her bleeding palms, absolutely unperturbed, unaware of the bloodshed she had saved. To her saving the animals for the pious act.

The signal turned green, the gates lifted, the animals lifted their trunks to pull down the branches, the vehicles honked their way across. Majoli lifted her ware basket with some effort as Rukhesh assisted. Anjini, pulled out a tube of cream from her sling bag to hand over to Majolie.

"O, my little kallu Kamla will be so happy with the cream, it's Apgaan Issnoo, na?"

The cyclists pedalled away, without answering.

The elephants sauntered into the ringal reeds, trumpeting to match the sounds of a metal track over run by metal wheels.

5

A Date on a Luxury Train

Nesten had begun the week by sending roses to Beverly.

She reciprocated the warmth with exotic chocolates, permitted a peck on the cheek, in return receiving a humongous oversized teddy, and a proposal to be his Valentine for life. The joyful response was the largest hug.

The entire week had been a surprise but the best one was reserved for the day itself. A unique trip to begin a lifelong journey. This Valentine's Day they're taking the luxury of spending a day making a trip on a luxury train from Beth to Lizzy and back via Queenie.

A slow, well decorated cabin, a reminder of the romance on the rails to the days back of Great-Grandpa and Great-Grandma, a hundred years ago. The romance of a century in the days post the turbulent days of the First World War and the horrors of influenza. Boys and girls born in the war, wanted to live in innocent, perfect, pure romance. A threat of more war did loom on the borders of Europe, but they chose to live in love. Those were the days when romance filled the countryside. Rose bowers, flower showers, evergreen trees, shaded pathways with ducks waddling in and out of ponds held the eyes as they rested far and near.

Riding on horseback, travelling in horse drawn carriages was the ordinary way but boarding a luxurious train was real romance.

A Valentine's Day luxury train tour on a luxury locomotive drawing the past century style carriage, well polished glass panes with lace curtains gently tied with satin ribbons in beautiful bows, was recreated for those in love by the HRHR.

Fine dining, a seven course meal, silver crockery and cutlery laid out in perfection with Belgian cut glassware to hold the seasoned, matured wines.

A fairyland dream, beyond the fertile imagination of the best animators, assembled together for those in love. Picture perfect not a strand out of place.

"Oh!! Nesten!!"

"Darling Beverly!"

"Magic, pure magic, I shiver as I imagine my Great-Grandma, dressed in her finest laces and ribbons, a new hat from the milliner, her handbag and sandals from Paris, what a luxury."

A band of strolling musicians walked past, playing the song 'I am in love'.

"I wish they would stop and play the entire song for us."

"Let's go and see what's happening at the magician's table."

A man deft in his craft, assisted by an equally clever woman, entertained the enthralled audience, who could not stop applauding the perfect performance.

The cards pulled out for Beverly and Nesten read "A match made in Heaven - Pure, Perfect Pair.

They looked into each other's eyes, smiled, interlocked their fingers and strolled to their cabin.

Returning to their sears they sank into the luxurious armchair in the beautiful white and gold designed coach.

"Dearest Nesten, let us enjoy this quality time" closing her eyes, Beverly extended her manicured fingers, imagining her loved one slipping a rose diamond onto her ring finger. She felt her hand lie between two comforting, warm palms, rubbing, soothing and caressing her soft skin.

"Dearest Nesten, is this true? Pinch me. No, no, let me dream, don't shatter this vision. Darling, thank you, thank you."

She opened her eyes, to see the glorious British countryside glide by.

Elms, willows, oaks, dotted with a lonesome maple standing with outstretched arms among the graceful pines, as the mist rolled in and out, for young people to enjoy apricity.

A steward walked in, a bubbling, cold champagne, a heartwarming word of greeting "Good day, Master and Greetings Mistress, we are honoured to travel with you. We are available for on-hand service, to assist you in every need."

"The pleasure is all our."

Beverly extended her elbow crook. Taking the clue, Nesten slipped his arm, to complete the ring bond. Raising the slender necked glass of champagne, the two uttered a toast

"To your health, to my health, to your long life, to my long life, to our health, to our long life we raise this toast." Taking a sip they continued "May we raise this toast, half a century later, surrounded by our tribe, symbol of our love forever."

"Honourable Master, Gentle Mistress you may call on anything you desire from our well-stocked bar." informed the steward as he returned.

Half an hour later, Nesten and Beverly were famished enough to enjoy a romantic seven-course lunch including a Great British cheese board, Indian curries, roast potatoes with mint lamb. The biscuits and chutneys were in no short supply. The highlight being a sundae ice cream with every texture, flavour and colour incorporated layer by layer, a treat for the eyes, tongue, palate and vibration of the eardrum.

A bottle of wine to compliment each couple along with the meal, while they presented a gift completed the Valentine experience.

"Close your eyes, Darling Nesten" whispered Beverly.

The man besotted by beauty, smitten by love, drowned in the romance, did as he was bid.

"Open your eyes" before him lay two sepia coloured photographs.

"Our Great-Grandparents, loved and married for over sixty years. In their presence, I accept the proposal you put forth two days ago, with hope that our great-grandchildren will share our photo with a loved one, a century down the line."

Nesten, switched on the mobile, stood behind her, slipped a rose diamond ring on her finger, clicking a selfie with the other hand.

She, shyly, took off a gold band from the chain around her neck and slipped it on Nesten's finger. The train halted, bringing a truly romantic and memorable day to a beautiful close.

The newly engaged Beverly and Nesten were already discussing the plans for the wedding day and a trip to follow on a luxury liner.

6

Death to Life and Beyond

Pronnomati was given a new posting to Prassmysl, as reporter for the Bharat Times. Delighted as a professional, a chance to grow, saddened as a parent of a ten year old.

"Maasaab, don't worry, I'll join you in November for the winter vacation, we'll see the Swiss snows, go to Venice and Christmas in Poland or Germany, as you say. I know you are a brave woman. You can do it."

"My boy, repeating my words to me." thought the reporter, while her husband Kreeshnan and parents-in-law, Abuja and Maaji assured her with similar words.

Two days later she was at the Prassmysl Railway Station, ready to interview people crossing over from Ukraine, facing a war, violence that destroys everything - nature, friendship, past relations, present and future hopes and aspirations.

The safe border of Poland was about a quarter of an hour minutes from the war border. The last railway station at the international line was built in the last decade of the nineteenth century in the neo-baroque style. Looking at the edifice she thought "The structure is taken care of. The artwork on display exhibits each line and curve clearly. The grand chandeliers are dusted and shine like brightly coloured tiles".

Pronnomati was not inspecting the building as a foreigner or tourist would do. She was seeing a crowd of people as she stepped down from the carriage. Hundreds of people, walking past tables full of coffee flasks, vats of soup and biscuit packets. Suitcases, blankets and plastic bags, overflowing with   packets of instant noodles and bread caught her attention.

At the other end of the table a young girl sat huddled in a blue sleeping bag. The reporter stopped to talk to her. Her voice was barely audible.

"Pull the bag around your legs. May I help you?"

"No, thank you. I am fine. I am wearing my stockings, it is Rover, my pet who is cold."

"Rover?"

"Yes, my pet. Can you see?" she said pulling back the cover, two large, black eyes peered through, a bit sad, as if they knew of the hard times ahead. Close by, lay a bag with dog feed.

"Dog feed? Dear."

"Yes, Rover must not go hungry, we don't know if my sponsor will adopt her. At least I can provide the food, till she settles with her new owner."

Another train rolled in, leaving more children and aged people to cross the border.

Helplessly, they looked around, searching for a place to sit.

Spotting an aged woman, old enough to be her grandmother, the reporter jogged to her as she walked slowly with the help of her walking stick. Taking courage, the young woman placed her palm over the bony fingers, adjusting her backpack on the shoulder. The elderly woman raised her head and gave a feeble smile.

"Hullo, where? from?"

"India."

"Good, India good, welcomed us long ago. Again, kind Indian. Studying?"

"No, I am reporting about Indians here, students, businessmen."

Hearing the word India, Indian, a group of young students from Asian countries huddled around me.

"Medical School?"

"Yes, only four months were left to go home."

"Second year."

"Waiting to join, learning the language."

The elderly lady was joined by another woman, carrying two paper cups of black, sugarless coffee

"Here, Caren, enjoy it before it turns bitter."

"My friend from Liev"

"I came across to take her to Karsew. She married in Liev, her son is going to war. Her daughter-in-law is bringing the grandchildren by the next train. No place today." explained the woman.

The chill was setting in, the dim lights cut through the curling vapours.

"Madam, from where in India?"

"M P, working in NCR."

"Any contacts?"

"Yes, Embassy."

"Please, please tell them to contact...+91....00" she rattled an Indian number. "Message, I am well."

"Name?"

"Sukirti". The reporter thought of her own son.

People were waiting, the counters and kiosks were closed. No one went to the restroom in the waiting room, not wanting to miss the call from the train across the border, never sure when a sponsor would come and take them.

Pronnomati boarded the returning train going to Liev. 'Into the jaws of Death' she thought 'rode the six hundred', the words played over, over again in her mind, or was it Valley 'Into the Valley of Death rode the six hundred' here she was alone, riding towards the war zone. As she sat on the moving train, staring into the darkness another line raced through " … . a long exile is your fate."

Her assignment was to meet people in Liev and return two days later. "But what? if not... ?"

There were three men, whispering to each other. They had left their family members to be picked up at the railway station. They were returning to fight against an unjust war forced upon them, on their land.

She caught a whisper "If we don't meet again... ." the remaining words were drowned in the rattling wheels on the tracks.

"Were the words for each other? or about the family they had left behind? and if I don't... ?"

"No, No" she shook her head "The son we hold in love. No, I have to return." The darkness seemed darker as large rockets flashed over.

Reaching Liev, she introduced herself to a woman sitting on a railway bench. Beside her, there were two large suitcases, a plastic bag filled with packed food and a large flask of black, sugarless coffee that would turn bitter if not consumed.

Next to her sat a young girl, her plait ribbons peeped out of her multi-coloured knitted cap, with a large wool bobbin.

She laughed, loudly, tugging at her parka, throwing her doll into the air and catching it before it touched the ground.

Her mother kept speaking all the while on her mobile, very fast, in a dialect that the reporter knew not.

The pretty girl, dragged her doll to the reporter

"Anni" she said pointing to the doll, "Barbie" she said pointing to herself. Probably the names had been interchanged. Keeping her finger on the reporter, she moved her tiny fingers, turning her wrist, to ask her her name.

"Pronnomati, Anni."

The child stuck out her tongue though the toothless gap "Anni"

The train whistle blew, a signal for it to leave.

Two women and a girl stood on the platform, as the three men went away in the moving train.

A rocket missile burst and flashed above them. The sirens warned to run for safety.

Death hovered all around, the living sought a life with hope beyond the dark.

7

 **Lest We Forget** 

The kind hearted Thai householders get up early each morning to give alms to at least five Buddhist monks. By tradition, the novices and monks visit five households only each day for their daily needs. They pick up a packet, their share, kindly prepared and placed on the table by a householder.

My host, Gurbani, an ethnic Indian, born in Pattaya, educated in India, married in Thailand, ran a country side resort, helping her husband, as her sons lived in Chicago.

She gets up religiously to cook fresh food for the visiting monks daily. Once the packets are ready, they are placed outside.

"Suwadee Kha"

"Suwadee Khap.", the traditional greeting is exchanged with a neighbour, also busy with the morning ritual.

It has been so ever since she returned to the land of her birth.

Three of her elder siblings moved here with her parents from the motherland. She, the youngest of a dozen children, was sent to study in a boarding school in India.

At the school, we grew up in mutual respect, I was in awe of her brilliant academic records, which I realized decades later was the result of her being older than us, her classmates, by at least three years.

A reunion hosted by the Bangkok Chapter, half a century later in Thonburi, saw us talking a score to dozen, as if not a day had passed in between since we last met.

"How come your family settled in Thailand? Leaving beautiful Punjab behind."

"No complaints, that we are here. We have done well. My siblings and their children have earned good money, respect and travelled places. But, like all good things, the beginning was hard, very hard."

"Oh, your family came by compulsion, not by choice."

"Ye, yes. My Father 'Darji' was a member of the British Indian Army. He was made a prisoner by the N'pyons."

"World War 2?"

"K'rect, hard task masters. They huddled all the young PoWs, to work on making a railway line from Siam to Baama."

"Myanmaar?"

"K'rect, eighteen hours, cut rocks, over the river, very fast, they aimed at reaching India."

"Cutting rocks, almost bare hands, cruel, little food, very little water, then cholera spread."

"Oh, no!"

"Oh, yes, work was not completed. The Japanese led the Dutch, British, Indians, Australian captives. Many were dying. Many important senior officers were also treated like everyday labour."

"Can we see the railway?"

"Some parts, yes, a museum is there. We can see it in a film or read about it in a book."

"Have you visited the museum? Can I visit it?"

"Uhmm, I was a little girl, youngest of all in the family, Darji told us many things, I understood little. He was too ashamed to live in his village in Punjab, thinking of himself as a prisoner of war. Thus, after his release from the rest camp, he brought Beeji and his three children here. He thought these people would understand his pain. He worked hard to begin life anew. Beeji supported him. Their effort paid off. Here I am!!" she smiled.

***

"Kanchanburi and visit to Hellfire Pass" Gurbani informed me two days later, "is the programme today."

The museum was divided into two parts, we were permitted to see the belongings, paintings and items used by the labourers who built the Death Railway. A thousand thousand died cutting the pass at Hellfire, a name given due to the shining torches as they worked and fell along with the exhausted workers.

Gurbani was silent through the entire journey, looking out and absorbing every fleeting scene.

One curve was so sharp, we could see both ends of the train at the same time.

She held my hand at different points in the journey, palms sweating, quivering, clutching saying something held in her heart. I did not understand the language but the emotion was crystal clear.

Later, when we got off the train, she stopped, held both my hands "Thank you, for bringing me here. I never had enough courage to take this journey over River Kwai, an unsaid fear held me back, I avoided it deliberately, but today a gap is bandaged. Thank you, Dear Friend."

A memory formed to release memories of another time, bridged by the Kwai Bridge.

8

Barog, Immemorable Tunnel

"O, Gosh, gosh, gosh" continued Piterson, Ray Piterson, standing on the engine, moving gently up the medium gradient. "Ooo, ooo, ... oo" he raised his arms "Ooo, ooyyee, ooo" he jumped down, ran back, and hopped on to his coach, holding the strong steel bar, leaning out, seeing the vegetation, pines, chir, oak, rhododendron, shrubs with simple flowers in shades of red and yellow.

The sky above a blue more than blue, curly, fluffy clouds over the mountain peaks shimmering in the bright sun.

He breathed deep, deep to inhale a whole lot of fresh air, the air of Barog, his great grandfather's village before it became a railway platform.

The prettiest of fairytale railway stations in blue and white, quaint wooden benches with arched pillars holding up the red roof made his heart beat faster than the speed of the train. His heart had begun to race as the engine, a reminder of the first Hill Puffer entering the longest, out of the hundred odd tunnels, is the Barog-Harrington tunnel.

The fellow passengers exchanged notes as they sat side by side

"Barog Saab roams up and down. Sit still, you may see him."

"Barog Saab, he was in-charge of the construction of this tunnel."

"He got the workers to drill from both ends, in hope of getting the work done quickly."

"Ok, they would meet in the centre."

"Yup, but it went wrong, the tunnels ended up parallel."

"Project delayed."

"No, triple engine!! Didn't Babaji help?"

"Exactly, *Sarkaar*, the British government was upset with the company, as the Viceroy, Lord Curzon, wanted to travel comfortably to the Summer capital."

"Simla was the Summer Capital, the entire *Sarkaari Taam Jhaam* travelled from Calcutta, on carts and carriages, till a private company offered to construct this narrow gauge Chuk Chug."

"Barog Saab was fined Rs 1/-, a token amount for wasting time and money."

"Re 1/-?"

"Big, big insult, a big fine, a matter of *izzat*. He couldn't take it, came here and shot himself, now roams up and down, see, see, there in his blue suit."

"His work was completed by engineer Harrington and Chail Baba."

The three minute ride was indeed spooky. Not one but many spirits seemed to occupy the tunnel, enjoying a ride on the fumes.

The Kalka-Simla-Kalka mountain train, a UNESCO heritage site, to reach the elevated ridge destination for the British, continues to run everyday.

With 920 curves, 969 bridges, 110 tunnels, and crossing 20 railway stations, the train takes anywhere between five to seven hours, running at regular intervals from both ends.

For Ray it was a journey of a life-time, a journey of ages. It was here that his Great-grandfather had been a station master. He stood looking at the grand railway clock, chiming, dutifully outside the Station Master's cabin.

"O, Dadu, it was here you walked, from time to time." He ran his hand over the stone lime wall, wondering how many times his Great-grandfather touched the wall.

Ray slung his backpack on to his shoulder, looked at his mobile, he had three hours to roam the town, before taking the train back to Kalka.

"Good old place, on my next visit, I will spend a week at least."

Who knows I may find Dadu's name scratched on a pillar, tree or wall somewhere or a file bearing his initials and signature.

9

A Train Wedding

You are cordially invited to attend the

WEDDiNG CEREMONY

of

Suryaprabha

(daughter of Smita and Ankleshwar of Jodhpur)

and

Prabhakaar

(son of Aljashree and Mauleshwar of Ambernagar)

on Sunday, February 2, 2025.

All attending guests must be present at the Departure Station, Jaipur by 14:00 hours, Saturday, February 1, 2025.

The Arrival for Homecoming is scheduled for Tuesday, 4 February, 2025, 18:30 hours.

The route undertaken will have stoppages at Udaipur, Nahargarh, Chottidhani, Sehari and Reshamnagri.

(A no pets policy will be strictly followed to avoid upsetting guests who may express a displeasure to fur, claws, licks, bounces, screeches and friendly bites)

Confirm your presence by, 30 September, 2024 along with a valid pc of coloured Aadhaar and pp sized front face coloured photograph.

Your personal presence, time and affectionate participation in the ceremonies shall be the life-long gift for the bride and groom.

Chaubeys and Mahaubes

=========

"How can we say No?"

"We are the common relatives to both families. Now they are becoming one family. They have always attended our family functions, even when Twinkle had exams and Raju Mumma was seriously ill, they took the trouble to attend. Refusal is out of the question."

"Anyway they have booked 32 carriages, the bare minimum required for a train wedding, if all are not occupied, it will be a shame."

Lovely and Sunny added their names to the guest list, sending the documents asked for immediately.

****

On the day of departure, Platform 22 - VST was all decked up in pink and gold to welcome each guest.

"Maharaj Saa, please take your seat... . .."* a welcome hostess in traditional Rajasthani ghagra, choli, laang and boor stood with folded hands, wearing silver jewellery.

"Maharani Saab..."

"Kunwar Saab..."

"Rajkumari Saab…"

One by one the guests were led to the retiring room while the stewards numbered and loaded the luggage.

Fruit juices, Rajasthani savouries, sweet dishes from every state of India were offered with *mukhwaas* and *paan*.

A *hookah* with a gold tip mouthpiece snout was ready for use as the customary folk music from rural desert lands soothed the ears.

The engine was decorated in marigolds interwoven with jasmine, roses and lotus buds.

Coaches 1 to 9 for the bride's guests, Coach 10 for the bride, her siblings and parents, Coach 11 as Pantry I, Coach 12 to 15 for assistance to the bride's family, Coach 16, the auspicious one for the ceremonies, Coach 17 to 21 assistance to the groom's family, Coach 22 as Pantry II, Coach 23 for the groom, his parents and siblings, Coach 24 to 30 for the groom's family. Coach 31 reserved for the couple, post the ceremonies.

Coaches from 32 to 41 reserved for the event managers, luggage, seamstress assistance, medical aid, theatre room, ballroom and a fully furnished bar.

"I am feeling like a real Maharana" said Grandfather twirling his moustache as the ceremonial turban was tied.

"I am no less, Mahrani, a Maharani" said the Grandmother adjusting her diamond *boor* and *lehariya chunari*.

The signal went down at 15:00 hours, with a huge cry of *"Jay, jay, badhai bhay, yatra shubhmaye"* the journey began.

As per the ritual programme *haldi rasm* was followed by *mehndi* ceremony. The decor was lit according to the ceremony in pale yellow and emerald.

Endless food was rolled out from the pantries, Rajasthani, Continental, Sino-Tibetan, Mexican and 'On Request' was readily available.

Musicians and dancers entertained non-stop, with the guests joining in joyfully, chattering, exchanging notes, catching up on finer details of family functions that they gad missed, due to preoccupation.

Stops came and went by unnoticed.

The time for the 'sapt padi' saw a rush to the ceremonial coach, others viewed it on the LED screens in their own coaches.

The bubbly, delightfully giggling girls, quietly hid the groom's footwear.

"*Jija Saab,* don't be a miser. Six of us, each deserves a gold chain."

"Done, but no shop here dears, return my shoes, please."

"No excuses, it is a request."

Someone broke into a Bollywood song about the exchange of footwear and money.

A smile crossed the bride's blushing cheeks, thinking how cheeky her sisters and cousins were acting. She thought of the scene enacted by the beautiful actress of past years, Madhoorijee.

"I wonder if I look half as pretty as her?" She raised her eyelids to look at the groom, he smiled and gave a thumbs up sign.

"Ah, Ma'am, can you please give us the same smile?" requested the videographer and photographer.

The bride shook, as the train ran over a joint on the track.

"Action replay," said the event manager.

The groom gave a sharp look to the unprofessional manager.

The bride threw a handful of puffed rice behind her, after taking the *pheras* around the sacred fire, protected in a large pyro-urn.

"Congratulations SuryaPrabhakar" glowed in every coach as the tiny rice lights lit up, in pink, green and blue glow.

Applauses, whistles, festive jumps and uncorking of champagne bottles, one after another continued way into the night, before the newlyweds could be led to their own reserved coach.

***

"O, my, to think I came on a mare, all the way to wed you." said GrandPa nostalgically.

"And I was given my farewell, *bidai* in the palanquin brought by you, with heavy curtains all around, and six palanquin carriers. How I cried all the way. Today, also, tears filled my eyes as Suryaprabha bid farewell to her parents. It is always such a touching moment."

"Be blessed, may health, prosperity, long-life companionship be granted for this journey that begins here." said the elders as Suryaprabhakaar, bowed before them.

10

Delights of an Overnight Journey

The Harrawala Railway Platform had a few passengers, awaiting the arrival of The Doon Express, on its way to Benaras.

All acquaintances from the same tiny town.

"Yes, going to Sandila, to meet my father."

"SSB, at Banaras, first option Air Force."

"Was here for Chandan's wedding. Love the place, but work calls elsewhere. Hmmm, posting is in Bareilly."

"The signal is down."

Martha got up from the wooden bench, next to the Wheeler's Book Stall. She had already purchased two magazines, Film World and Who's Who, in anticipation of reading them, as she found it difficult to converse to strangers.

Coach S-6, berth 22.

She ran behind the porter carrying her trunk and holdall. The man in his brown turban, maroon kurta, once upon a time white dhoti, raw leather chappals with the bronze railway tag tied on his arm, arranged her luggage carefully.

"Here, I don't have change." she said handing over the blue currency note.

The porter dug into the upper pocket, of his sweat wet kurta, on the left hand side, with a pure silver 100 gm bracelet on his right hand to return the remaining amount.

"Check your luggage, count three items, two on the berth, one below."

The train began to move.

Martha sat down, looked out of the dusty, stained pane, she could see her house in the distance.

Two children, aged five and seven, pushed their little heads, to peep out.

"Madam ji, sorry, they want to see the tracks running back, Kittu, Kitty, don't trouble Madam ji, behave, and come back to your berth in two minutes." said the father.

Leaving the children, he went back to help his wife who was trying to spread the bedding on the upper berth.

"Madam ji, where are you going?"

"Where are you going?"

"Benaras, Papa has a job there. But where are you going?"

"Beneras, I also have a job there."

"Teacher or Doctor?"

"No, Magistrate."

"Majistrat? What does a majistrat do?"

"What does a magistrate do? lots of work, work for the people."

"Lots of work, Mumma also does a lot of work. Cooking, ironing, sending us to Balvari, talking, seeing TV,.. and"

".. And making my favourite samosas, and gajar halva."

Kitty ran to her mother "Mumma, give me halva, I won't give it to Kittu. I will give you, I will give Papa, I will give Madam ji."

"Come on up, and sleep here, call Kittu, time to eat and sleep."

"No, the train is shaking, I will fall, I am going back, to see the station, bring the halva."

The train jerked and halted.

MOTICHUR

"*Garam chai*"

"*Channey, chutnee*"

"*Besan ladoo*"

"No, no, we have our aloo puri, mango pickle and dahi, Come Kitty, Kittu. Please join us, Madam."

"No, thank you. I don't like eating on a train" said Martha, as she gulped a mouthful of water from her water bottle. Unrolled her blanket and pulled it up to her shoulders, after tucking her shoes, wrapped in a plastic bag towards the side of her berth.

There was little sound of talking as most passengers settled on their berths.

Five boys dressed in T-shirts, with initials of their college, embroidered on the back, boarded the compartment, followed by a frail woman holding on to her bundle of clothes, tied in a blue bedsheet.

"Amma, which berth?"

"See, help me." the woman said, offering her ticket.

"That one."

"No, this one."

"Look at the number, 3 or 8?"

"Someone is sleeping, wake them."

"Amma, give us money, then I will help."

"Please, help, I have only a few rupees, very little money."

"Whatever, hand it over or I will tear the ticket."

"Give or here goes your ticket." said one beginning to tear the paper.

"Boys, stop troubling her. Have some shame."

"Madam, stay out of this. Is she your Grandmother?"

"Madam, let them be. I can manage without money."

"Hidden money, Amma? Here goes your ticket." The boys laughed menacingly passing the paper to each other.

The woman caressed the roll of currency notes before giving it to the boy who had the ticket.

The boy dangled the ticket before her face and then let it fall to the floor, pushing the wad of notes into his pocket.

"Let's pull the chain and stop the train." A loud laughter resonated over the clanging wheels and tracks.

As the train screeched to a halt, the T T C in his smart, dark blue uniform came in, followed by the R P

"Who pulled the chain?"

"Amma." laughed two boys.

"Amma, she is neither strong nor tall enough to pull the chain, speak the truth, if there is no valid reason, you pay a fine and get down."

"Well, I did because Amma requested and we respect and obey aged people. She wants to get down."

"Amma, say what happened. Do you want to get down?"

Offering the ticket to the T T C, she said "I have to travel till Mirzapur. Yes, I asked this boy to pull the chain."

The boys' faces brimmed with sadistic grins. Old woman, too scared to speak. Now she will have to get down.

"Amma, stopping a train for no reason is a crime, you will have to pay a fine."

"Yes, Saab, Please, check this boy's pockets, he snatched my money, check his shirt pocket. Because of the theft I had the chain pulled to stop the train."

"Oo, it's my money." cried the boy.

"Ask him, what's the amount? How many green notes, how many orange ones, how many blue pieces?"

"As if you can tell."

"Yes, I can, it is all of my savings for a year of hard work. Three green notes, six orange ones, five blue pieces, three thousand two hundred, I spent three blue ones for the ticket and some tea."

The T T C with the help of the railway police, recovered the money, tied in a rubber band, exactly as described by Amma. The boys were forced to disembark since five had planned to travel on a single ticket, in hope of using the toilet as their refuge.

Martha observed the incident making a mental note of the woman's wisdom, as she went back to her berth to sleep peacefully.

11

रेलगाड़ी

रेलगाड़ी, रेलगाड़ी

पहने तू नीली साडी

चलती तू छक, छक

आवाज़ आती धक धक

ले जाती तू दूर दरस्त

यात्री रहते व्यस्त मस्त

खाते पीते हँसते गाते

करते लम्बी लम्बी बातें

खिड़की से देखो दुनिया

प्यारी बिटिया मुनिया

पीछे रह जाते घर, पेड़

खम्बे, सड़क, खेत, मेड़

आता है कोई कहता 'चाय'

गाता है कोई 'हाय' 'बाय'

तेज़ी से आगे बढ़ती रेल

सुपर फास्ट हो या मेल

भिडम भाड़, धक्का मुक्की

रात दिन कभी ना रेल रूकी

चढ़ते उतरते अनेक यात्री

बढ़ती अनजानों से मैत्री

दुख में, सुख में ले जाती रेल

जोड़ती बढ़ाती सामाजिक बेल

अपने गंतव्य पहुंचाती गाड़ी

घुमाती हरी भरी सुंदर वादी

रेलगाड़ी तेरा आभार

तू करती नदी नाले पार

तेरी चाल भाती सब को

थके यात्री जल्दी जाते सो

कुछ घंटे में बनते मित्र

खींचते साथ में चित्र

यादें मन में समेट

छोड़ते स्टेशन गेट

आवाज़ आती धक धक

चलती तू छक, छक

पहने तू नीली साडी

रेलगाड़ी, रेलगाड़ी

12

School Party Travel by Train

Miss Thelva Camton, Camty, was at her busiest.

'Box checking' the annual ritual, of ensuring that each and every clothing item is duly packed in the black painted trunk, 6x4x2, with the name, class and cities painted in white.

Asgar Farokhi

Class VII

Patna-Doon-Patna

St. Anthony's (I) College

Asgar had been travelling by school party, since he was in Class IV.

Mr. Hubert Khite, would escort the boys on this route.

Winter vacations would begin three weeks later.

The trunks after a thorough box checking would be booked a week in advance, on the goods wagon, to ensure the trunks would be available in time for the boys to take home from the home station.

Casty, Miss Campton, could afford to make no mistakes, shirt collars repaired, buttons in place, hems perfect, every item washed, ironed, counted, listed, packed neatly was her pride. She just couldn't let down the name of the school.

One by one, the students would cross-check to sign the list. After all, now they were responsible for answering questions put to them about the school clothes.

"Big boy! all right?"

"Yes, Ma'rm" the perfect stress in a school aiming at perfection.

The porters carried the trunks to the out agency wagon. The trunks gone, just six more nights and the boys would leave.

"A little heavy on the heart, the devils trouble all the time, but I'll miss the angels. Travel safe... . and pack the trunks neatly, when you bring them back." mulled the matronly figure.

A week later, the immaculately dressed boys boarded the buses, party wise

"Amritsar"

"Delhi"

"Lucknow"

"Patna"

"Howrah"

"Bombay"

"Jhansi"

The boys in the Patna bus waited excitedly for Mr Khite but instead Padre Ganon, an Irish gentleman, a relatively short, snowy haired, Maths teacher, in his spotless white soutan, with a pale sash came in.

"Boys, unfortunately the favoured Mr Khite has been held back due to family commitments, hence I, a chronic bachelor, devoted to the spiritual life, shall join you. Remember, Padre Ganon, your priest, is the man who shall hand you over to your parents. You shall take Padre Ganon's permission to move from your berth, no naughtiness, no disobedience. Is that clear?"

Twenty sweet voices, aged nine to sixteen answered in unison "Yes, Padre."

"Is that clear?" the question was repeated

Twenty voices, aged sixteen to nine answered in unison "Yes, Padre."

The bus left the boys at the red bricked, arched entrance to the station.

Twenty boys, aged nine to sixteen, marched in immaculate uniforms to occupy their births.

"One, two, … . ten… sixteen,…nineteen, twenty."

"No movement, without permission. Is that clear?"

Twenty sweet voices, aged nine to sixteen answered in unison "Yes, Padre."

The train chugged out, the lights were left behind.

"Lights out. To sleep. Out of the blanket, sharp at 7. Is that clear?"

Twenty sweet voices, aged nine to sixteen answered in unison "Yes, Padre."

"Good Night."

"Good Night." responded twenty sweet voices, aged sixteen to nine.

The lights were dimmed.

The train wheels hit the rail metal, the whistle was sharp and shrill. Silence, the speed was high, the sound of howling wind whistled hitting against the metal body.

An apparition was moving, removing the blanket to check the faces on the berth.

"Help, save, save, Ooo, ghhhh…. ooo…. help" screamed the face on Berth Fourteen.

"Where, Whooii, whoo, .."

"Shut up, be quiet… q"

"Ghoooo…. oost."

"Nothing… all hoax.. be quiet."

"Don't move without permission. Is that clear?"

"Who is imitating me?" said the Padre's hoarse voice. "Go to sleep, don't move."

The apparition moved, berth to berth, removing the blanket to see the face on each berth.

"Ghooo…. st… gh… st."

The apparition lay down on berth, 21.

An Irish gentleman, relatively short, snowy haired, Maths teacher, in his spotless white soutan, with a pale sash spoke

"Don't move. Is that clear?"

Twenty sweet voices, aged nine to sixteen answered in unison "Yes, Padre."

"Ghhhh... .. oooo... stttt" said the voice on Fourteen.

13

Vendor Ware

"Be ready, it's your first day. The train will halt for two minutes, get in fast. People will be spilling their baggage and coming out, but you get in. Hold your basket tight." the experienced vendor instructed the novice.

"Yes, Bhau."

"Don't slip below the carriage and if the slipper slips out don't try to bend and get it, buy one when you have the money."

"Jee, Bhau."

The engine raced past, coach five before the novice and his mentor."

"Get in, get in."

Two women with large bags stood at the train gate. A railway porter was trying to enter to catch a customer.

The novice, Gagni, took an acrobatic jump, past the porter, the women into the alley.

Singing in a high pitched voice, with the basket resting on her waist, she began to sell the fried, rice pappads, painted pink with red chille dust.

The train chugged out gently before catching the full speed.

"₹ 10/ - per piece."

"Two for ten?"

"Please buy one, my first day. I have to pay for my licence."

"Is it fresh?"

"Made yesterday, fried today."

"Two pieces." the customer said, offering a five hundred rupee note.

"No change, It's my first sale."

"Sorry, PayPal? G-pay?"

Gagni moved ahead, without answering.

"₹ 10/ - per piece."

A kind hearted woman passenger purchased five, paying the right amount.

A smile crossed the vendor's face.

"Something is better than nothing." She thought of her mother who had diligently made each papad, in the last two days. Most of all, Bhau helped her get the licence and permission to vend her ware between Sitagarhi and Maghimandir, with a monthly pass.

"₹ 10/ - per piece." she sang again, the train had begun to slow down. Passengers began to push to get down.

"₹ 10/ - per piece."

"Move, keep your basket out of the way."

"Sorry, sorry" she said, trying to squeeze aside as people began to clamber in the narrow aisle.

"₹ 10/ - per piece." she sang gently.

"₹ 10/ - per piece."

"Try to sell something else, who eats papad. Fryum, finger cups, cheese balls, chutney chips."

"₹ 10/- per piece."

"₹10/- per piece." She sang repeatedly.

The train caught speed again.

"One, please."

"Two, please."

"One with less chilly."

"Find one with more chilly, yes, that's the one."

"₹ 10/ - per piece."

"Excuse me, can I make a short video?"

"Video?"

"Yes, I am a You-tuber, blogger, vlogger and influencer. Your sales will go up. Everyone on this route will purchase your ware."

"Ok, what do I have to do?"

"Sing as you have been doing."

"₹ 10/ - per piece. ₹ 10/ - per piece. Lovely, home-made, fresh, ₹ 10/ - per piece."

"Nice, would you like to see the recording?"

"Yes" she couldn't believe that she was seeing herself, her ware and hearing her voice.

"Is that me?"

"Of course, now sing. Buy three get one free. Do you think it's Ok?"

Gagni counted on her finger

"No, one free on five is Ok."

"You know your business, now sing, Buy five, get one free. The best *pappad* from Gagni, that's me."

"Here, listen and see" said the videographer.

"Vow! now what?"

"I will post it after editing, check on You-tube Channel, Vendor Wares."

"What is that?"

"Do you have a mobile?"

"Bhau has, he allows us to use it."

"Tell him, You-tube, Vendor Wares. Check Vendor Wares, tomorrow, you will be a hit, sales will soar."

"₹ 10/ - per piece." Gagni sang.

On reaching Maghimandir, Bhau, appeared from nowhere.

"Get down, your pass works till here, Move to Platform 5, take the overhead bridge, no crossing tracks. Take the next train back."

"N you?"

"Coming, the train VB-252 will come in half an hour, I will try to sell something here and join you."

"Bhau, someone, a beautiful girl made my video. She said I'll be on You-tube."

"Which Channel?"

"Ooo, ooo, Where, When, something, When door Where."

"Ok, I will check. Who was the creator? Name?"

"Don't know."

"Run along, don't miss the train and get down at Sitagarhi. Any sale?"

"Yes." she displayed her income.

"Keep the money out of sight, a pickpocket is watching carefully, she is ready to snatch it."

Gagni laughed, "Bhau, my chilli spray is ready." she said, tucking the money in her waist wallet.

She took the stairs leading to Platform 5, humming a soft tune "The day begins, the day ends, say the walking hens.

We peck, we deck, we stick out our neck.

The train comes, the train goes

Where? When? How? noone knows."

14

The Train is Late

"Hullo, What time is the Fazilka-Hoshiarpur starting?"

"The announcement says two hours, the message from the Railways says more than three."

"Shall we rest in the waiting room?"

"No, Thank you, I am fine, I enjoy the railway platform. You can join me for a cup of tea at the Kulhad Chai Stall."

"Indeed nothing like the aroma and taste of clay in tea."

"Please look after my bag and roll, I'll bring the tea, sugar or without sweetness?"

"Without sweetness."

"Diabetes? Sugar?"

"No, my life is sweetless, any amount of sweet is not going to sweeten it, so best tea also without sweetness."

"Why so bitter?"

"Long tale, let's cut it short, you watch the luggage, I'll bring the tea. Would you like it sweetened?"

"Nay, na, bland is fine. Bland."

"Hmmm, In the journey of life... hmmm... it is cold, damm me to forget wearing my gloves... Hmmm.."

"Thank you. How much do I owe you?"

"Welcome. Nothing."

"Not done, I can't take a free-bee from a stranger."

"No, not to worry."

"These railway people, they make lovely tea, food and even the environment is enjoyable."

"True, you know, many people's lives change completely on the railway platform."

"This platform has changed so much from the time I last came here."

"Yes, they have renovated and up graded it several times, the whole place was done up last year for G-20."

"Means? You come here often?"

"It is my home station. My parents live here, so as soon as I get leave time,..straight here."

"Leave that means, working elsewhere or from home, on-line work?"

"From my business. Woollen hand-knitted garments."

"Excuse me, hand-knitted garments. Did someone come to meet you, for a wedding proposal here, thirty two years ago?"

"Yes, very often, the person interested in marrying me or their relative, would observe me carefully as I got on or off the train, to check my public behaviour, walk, dress sense and all that. It was common back then, railway platform meetings. But why are you asking?"

"Well, I don't know if you recall, I happened to be one of them. Thirty two years ago. We met briefly, before you took the train."

"I do, as your response was, 'No way, no spectacles, I will not marry a spectacled one' isn't it?"

"Yes, but now I see, you aren't wearing spectacles and I have been wearing a pair for the last twenty five years."

"I don't need spectacles, those were for style, but that put me out of style."

"I apologize, did you finally marry and set up a family?"

"No, that was my parents dream and pet project, I am jolly, happy, single, busy, busy with my work. What brings you here? "

"An old friend, the one who requested me to meet you. Will you bring sweetness in my life and tea? I never found the perfect recipe for good tea, so I stopped pursuing the matter."

"The train is too late. The fog is thickening, I don't think it will start today. Tomorrow is another day. I better go home before I catch a chill. The train is late."

"Dear Passengers, due to heavy fog, Fazilka-Hoshiarpur Train Number 8052, is too late for departure. It has been cancelled. The railways regret the inconvenience."

"Bye, Thanks for the tea."

"You are welcome. No need for thanks, I did owe you one, since you bought one for me at our last meeting."

15

Late for the Train

"Excuse me, when is the wedding reception?"

"Whose?"

"Whose? as if we have been invited to a hundred. Pillu Bua's, daughter, Montu."

"Friday, the 13 th. December. "

"Sure? Are you sure?"

"Here, look at the card and read carefully.

Friday, 13 December, 2019.

Galaxay Gardens

Empire Orchid

Habsigauda."

"Ok, I am busy checking on the monitor, dearie, at least do this little thing."

"Friday, 13 December.

Non A C

lower sleeper

Sandip Coomar - male - age, 42

Randeep Coomar - female - 42 years.

Happy, dearie."

"Thanks dear, so we leave on 12th, attend the function and return by the same train."

"Reservation confirmed by Belundrabad - Habsigauda. This on-line booking is so convenient."

"Yes, Thank you. One thing off the list. Now the packing."

"Yes, this was a worry, we've got the seats we wanted. Travel safe, enjoy the trip."

"Family time is fun time, little pleasures, leg pulling, memories. I am waiting to meet Dadima, she always has so much say, cutie, cutie."

***

"Bye Sandip, Bye Randeep. Really, Thanks for coming. Such fun. Have you taken the box of sweets? See you soon. *Ammaji* is insisting that we visit you in June."

"Good idea, good, most welcome. We had a really memorable time. Every arrangement, too good. We'll wait for you."

"If the train is late, come back and wait here. Why sit in the retiring room?"

"Just checked at the enquiry, it's on time. Bye. Thanks."

"Bye."

***

"The signal has gone down, non A C sleeper coach will stop here, see the board."

"Come, come, remember, berth 5 and 8. Come."

"Excuse me, this is our berth."

"No, excuse me non A C sleeper coach, S-5, berth, 5 and 8, booked for us."

"Ours,..."

"Seee...ee, December 13, Friday. S-5."

"Hold on, what did you say, December 13, Friday, ha... ha... ha"

"Stop it, pick up your bags, we need to settle down."

"Ha,...ha... ha, ha... you mean get down. Get down before the train moves and you are fined for travelling in a reserved coach without a ticket."

"Here is our ticket, see, look at this."

"*Bapuji,* also said this, but he was hurled out, you better get down respectfully."

"What is going on? T T... T.. Teee.. Is there anyone here."

"Don't shout for T T, get down yourself. Today is Saturday, 14 th December. The time is 00:12 hours. The train shall depart at 00:15 hours. You have two minutes to get down. O ya, don't forget to buy a platform ticket before going out."

"Sandip, get down."

"Randeep, I want to laugh and cry. What shall I do?"

"Get down, then we'll decide."

"Ha, ha, ha... have a nice day. Bye."

16

The Underground Railroad Escape to Freedom

Cobalt Cobbsen, a slave for life working for Charles Cobbs, a cotton and sugarcane farmer and a slave driver.

The two about the same age lived diametrically contradictory lives, one of abject poverty, the other knew nothing but luxury; one with no free will, the other did as he wished and willed. One lived under a wall less half falling thatched roof while the other owned mansions.

The one thing in common was they had fathered almost the same number of children.

The youngest child of Charles, Yvonne was often taken by her maid to the fields. Her older siblings were busy with their city, social lives. Her Mother, too, was too tired to pay attention to her all the time. She enjoyed the outdoors. Her neighbour, Francis Drumpe also played around there. They grew up together, seeing the slaves working endlessly. The children would run around and break into a chattery, curious conversation. The communication was in gestures as there was no common language.

Cobalt and the other slaves often sang a sweet song in Afrikaans, as if mocking the horrors of their fate in its face.

Yvonne and Francis, sang along, clapping their chubby little hands, enjoying the sweet sound

***

Yvonne and Francis took the vows to spend all their days together, with a warmth for humanity.

They were against slavery and supported the abolitionists.

"Dear Francis, we have to open our home to the Underground Railroad."

"Darling Yvonne you have given words to my deepest feelings, but we have to be very careful. Even a whisper can mean trouble for the UgRr. Be cautious, Darling, not merely careful."

Yvonne sat doing her embroidery, looking up in between to see the chapel being built across the pathway. The workers worked one brick at a time. "Tomorrow shall take them to Freedom. They will be replaced in disguise, by another set of slaves attempting to escape."

Her chain of thoughts was stirred by

"Knock, Knock"

"Good Day, Mister Drumpe."

"Afternoon, afternoon Marshall Stuartt. What brings you here, at this hour? Come, come in."

"Slaves, Master Francis, you are sheltering runaway slaves."

"Sit, Marshall, sit. Slaves? Sheltering slaves. Come have a drink."

"No, Master Francis, I am on duty and in uniform. No drinks. I have my doubts and there will be no sparing if any runaway slaves are found in your shelter."

"Marshall, I know you do your duty, dutifully. I will not stop you. Do as you deem fit."

"Be warned, don't ever say 'Marshall Stuartt is an unfair officer'."

"Nay, never, neither an unfair officer nor an unfair man."

The guest left, using his baton on the furniture and door. The wife standing on the threshold spoke

"Dear Francis, are you sure, we can get the runaways to safety."

"Absolutely, we shall. Tomorrow is the day of rest, be rest assured our ride to the prairies, will do the needful. Thomas Jeffer will keep his word, he is a faithful human."

***

Yvonne sat doing her embroidery, she looked out of the window. The chapel was complete, over eighty slaves had worked and escaped by using the work site as a station.

"Now what? Dear Francis says we will add a new wing to our mansion to continue our work of Underground Railroads."

Her chain if thoughts was stirred

"Knock, knock"

"Who do you want? What is your name?"

"Me name, Feather Cobbsen, I wish to see Mester Francis or Mestress Yvonne."

The Mistress of Drumpe Mansions, walked to the back door.

"Ahoy, Missus, ahoy. Praise be to the Underground Railroads, and you and the Mester be one of them."

"Shhh, Cobbsen, shhh, we are under watch, have a drink and hot bun and go."

"Nay, to worry, President Abe Lincoln have signed the instrument of freedom for all slaves. We are free. Thanks to all Underground Railroad members, who gave us shelter, who let their home be a station for our escape. Ahoy, Mestress, ahoy."

Francis Drumpe walked, holding his head in pride, his effort along with that of his fellow Underground Railroads, the work in secrecy of so many years in helping slaves to escape had been fruitful.

The abolitionists, Underground Railroads had brought about a revolution, without wheels.

Marshall Stuartt stood at the chapel gateway, equally proud that he had helped by making no report though he had every bit of evidence to prove that Yvonne and Frances were Underground Railroad assistants.

17

Railway 200

Travelling from Rishikesh to Silkyara, to see the tunnel under construction, Anveeta was all jitters and butterflies filled her stomach. The ride was long, looking down at the valley, with the river flowing in serenity, was not enough to calm her.

"Railway tunnel, Papa. Is it very long and high?"

"Yes."

"How much?" she questioned curiously.

"Very, you will see when we reach there?"

A minute later, she posed a new question

"Papa, where did the railway come from?"

"England."

"England? Can we go there?"

"Yes."

"How? on a train?"

"By aeroplane or by ship."

"Let's go."

"We are going."

"When? Today?"

"No, in September, to participate in Railways 200."

"200? 200 means?"

"Like you are six years old, you were born in 2019. Railways-Locomotives were born in 1825."

She began to count on her little fingers.

"One, two, three, six, nine, twelve, fifteen… . thirty, … . forty five,…sixty… , seventy five… . ninety… . . one hundred and… .. now what?"

"Two times one hundred."

"I want to see the first train.'

"Ok, we can see it in the museum, you can see it here." said the father, playing a video on his mobile.

The child watched the video with good intent.

"Papa, first the railway had no engine, horses pulled it."

"Correct, horse power."

"Not for people, but to carry coal."

"Yes, coal for making iron."

"Then came a steam engine. used on 25 September, 1825."

"Vow"

"Yes, when we visit England in September, we'll see, as it was. Five hundred passengers, reporters on the way. People, lots, it was a holiday."

"What fun, sitting on the first train, horses running, which place?"

"Darlington to Stockton."

"Can we sit on that train?"

"Hmm, we could try, at least try to take part in some events, you could win a prize or a certificate."

"Events?"

"Events, like poster making, photography, vadges, slogans, drawing, painting, skits, history quiz."

"See so much, people were so happy with railways?"

"Yes, a big invention, style of travel changed. People went to see new places."

"But some places never got trains, like our hills."

"Yes, it was difficult to cut the rocks. Very difficult to bring the material, broad gauge not possible."

"O, can I be a loco pilot? or loco engineer and make a train easy for hills."

"Why not? One must dream and fulfill one's dreams."

"Let me sleep and dream, wake me up at the tunnel."

"Dream, dream big and fulfill the dream.'

18

Bombay Locals

Harbans had lived in a remote settlement in Gopeshwar. Against his wishes, his son, Veer had brought him to Bombay, after he lost his wife. Veer worked in the Colaba Vegetable Market and lived in a shanty house near the track. Harbans saw the trains running all day and heard them late into the night and early in the morning.

The only time he had sat in a train was when he travelled to Bombay.

One day, having nothing much to do, he got onto a train.

He looked around, a bustling town, nay city, no metropolitan with so many suburbs. Having a long history, a complicated geography with the metro trains acting as the arteries and veins, The Bombay Central it's heart. Managing hundreds of 'Up and Down' trains.

Jam packed with people and more people, Locals, residents, tourists, professionals, site-seers, people earning a living on the train, people living off the train, people working for the train. People in a hurry, not to miss the local.

Fisher women, garland makers, the dabbawalas, pav bhaji sellers, chai, coffee, tiffin service, families, strangers, all on the train, crowded or in a vacant coach.

Women sitting and shelling the peas, chopping cauliflowers, handling children, holding onto milk cans, singing-dancing troupes coercing money from hapless newly weds or cursing in high pitched voices.

Many more standing, packed liked pickled sardines, anxiously looking at the display board hoping to reach the exit and walk out safely.

Harbans finally found a place to look out of the window. Tracks and tracks crossing each other.

His mind raced, how does the loco pilot know which one to take? The goat paths in the grassy hills were, are so much easier. Wires, water pipes, overhead bridges and houses along the tracks, shanties-tin, plastic, asbestos, wood, glass assembled to resemble walls, roofs and courtyards. Antenna, TV dishes, mobile towers and skyscrapers in the background. Billions of people escaped from open, fresh aired, large spaces gathered here. All arriving here in trains, with and without tickets.

Children running, playing in the narrow alleys, dangerously close to the tracks, in mere tatters joyfully waving to the heads and eyes in the train window.

"See, see, she has taken my bag."

Two burly men caught a wisp of a girl, with matted hair tied in a dirty ribbon and gave two hard punches on her back. She fell to the train floor. The peanuts held in a newspaper scrap fell out of her hands, only to be crushed by the shoes of the passengers.

"Where is the bag?" a fat man asked, shaking the girl by the shoulder.

She rolled over, took a quick flip and slid away. The fat man tried to push his way, but the girl was gone.

The fat man turned to locate his own bag.

In shock and anger, he looked around, seeing Harbans, he caught him by the collar

"You were sitting here, who took my bag? Or you are part of the gang."

"Gang? What gang? What happened?"

"Don't act innocent, you all disguised as simpletons, helpless passengers, ride this metro, taking advantage of the crowd, eye our baggage. Speak up, where is your accomplice? Police, Police."

Astounded, Harbans sat frozen, a tear rolled down. He sniffed and closed his eyes.

"Get up, don't sit here. And get off at the next stop. You are looking at us strangely. Why are you here?"

"A, aa, I..." Harbans stammered as he was not very familiar with the dialect. Someone pushed him towards the exit.

He stood crushed by the crowd. Shifting from foot to foot, he held a hand sling, swaying with the train.

"Trring...trriing"

The fat man swiped the mobile screen to take the call.

"Hullo, ..yes, yes,...black bag, with my name and phone tag......Thank you. I thought someone stole it...Please keep it. I will pick it tomorrow."

He laughed sheepishly,

"Here, take your chain. It is not real gold?" he said, handing it back to Harbans.

"Ha, ha, I unhooked it as I held your collar. Sorry, ya, Lost and Found just phoned to say they found an unattended bag on the platform. The phone tag helped them contact me. No hard feelings, fella. Hope we meet again."

Harbans thought to himself, "Never again!" Why do we have to leave our homes? To be manhandled by these goons. "I am going back, better off without a train, just walking."

19

Mind the Gap, Mind Your Head

"Hullo, Doctor" said a squeaky voice.

"Good Evening, please take your seat."

She looked up and was surprised to see a smart gentleman, steady and strong.

"Thank you." the voice cracked.

"How may I help you? What ails you? Sore throat?"

The man nodded, rubbing hischeek and throat.

"Painful?"

The man tended to agree, finding it hard to swallow the saliva. The pain was evident on his face.

She wore her gloves and face mask, took her battery torch, and switched it on.

"Please come to the chair." the dentist said, pointing to the reclining chair "Open your mouth." The dentist's attendant adjusted the head rest, lighting for the head."

She peered deep into his mouth and throat. The larynx wobbled.

"Thank you, Mind Your Head, O, Mind the Gap, rotten tooth. Rest, no talk, take steam and gargle, and wash the cavity with saline lukewarm water, thrice a day."

The man pursed his lips, smiled, took the prescription, bowed and walked away.

Three days later, Nicheo Biegat walked in to meet his doctor, Cathy McOpenner, at the appointed time.

"Hullo, Mr Biegat, how do you do? How's your throat, let me check the tooth."

"Nicheo, Doctor, cured, all well. The rotten root gave way, just fell out. "

Doctor McOpenner was taken aback on hearing the sound, what a voice? a playback, public address voice.

"I am glad, you are well. I must compliment your voice, it sounds familiar, are you on the radio?"

"No, Doctor, It's recorded for 'Mind the Gap, Mind Your Head' announcement at Deargeo Garden Tube Crossing. Maybe you've been there."

"Yea, sometimes, I go help at St. Veetur Dental Hospital, and yes of course, I have been guided by 'Mind the Gap. Mind Your Head.' warning, even saved twice from an accident. Thank you."

"Thank you, Doctor. May I have the pleasure of taking Cathy for a coffee today, post her day."

Cathy was pleasantly surprised by this request. For years, she had called it a day and gone to an empty nest, that it had been so forever.

"Coffee? I work till 7:30."

"Dinner then."

"Are you sure? It won't be a trouble?"

"Yes, sure, no trouble. You can hear the recording at Deargeo Garden Tube Crossing, at Cafe named after the announcement 'Mind the Gap, Mind the Head' - Cafe MGH.

Arriving at the Crossing, in the Tube Tram, in time to hear 'Mind the Gap, Mind the Head', heading to Cafe MGH.

Ordering the dinner after a close scrutiny of the menu, they exchanged details of their lives.

An hour later Nicheo offered his lifelong companionship to Cathy, who accepted the proposal without a second thought.

Time and again, especially on favourite days they would visit Cafe MGH to bloom in each other's company.

Nicheo's voice recording, was embedded deeply in her mind, a soothing phrase and sound she often repeated to her patients.

"I was all of seventeen years, when the warning was recorded. Out of the many, who participated, mine was found to qualify in diction, clarity and a clear intonation, so here I am, my voice, repeating it every twenty seconds, the expected average time for a passenger to go past, over twenty years now."

On one of the couple's visit, a mechanical voice repeated the warning,

'Mind the Gap. Mind Your Head.'

"O Nicheo, this is not your voice. This is too cold, no warmth. Khut, khut, khat, no, no, I'll get your voice back."

"Ha, ha,.....Rest, no talk, take steam and gargle, and wash the cavity with saline lukewarm water, thrice a day, the suggested recipe when we first met."

"Gosh, you remember and recall it word for word, Dearest Nicheo."

"I heard them, bringing the love of my life to me."

Cathy blushed, searched the number for the competent authority, messaged her request for the human voice.

The gentle officer, moved by the plea, accepted the request, had a CD cut and sent it to the loving wife, so that she could play it whenever she wanted.

20

Friends for Ever

Telsang lived in the mountains, the home of the Snows. His parents, Lobsang and Pembu, helped in the Hermeer Monastery, home of the Gayla Lama and his pupils. The monastery had room for ninety young boys, currently, its occupancy was seventy.

The rock mountains, with hardly any vegetation, rose sharply reaching the blue skies. The peaks were snow capped and turned orange, pink, golden and yellow before the moon changed it into a flowing gown of silver, till the dawn painted it pink again.

Sometimes, a bright green helicopter would whirl around, breaking the silence, dominating over the chant of *'aum mani padmani hum'* that filled the monastery air throughout the day.

The novices in the monastery were five year to seventy years olds. Most of them had walked up the winding hill path, some had come on yak back.

They were searching for something beyond this mortal world. Their dedication to a life of celibacy, barely with any needs, was in stark contrast to the world seen on screen.

Telsang saw many new places and strange things on his father's new device, a mobile phone, gifted to him by his cousin, Limbu, who lived in the USA.

Chachey Limbu, had been taken to the USA, thirty years ago by an American disciple of Gayla Lama.

Telsang was fascinated by all the wonders out there, everything was magical but the train running on tracks held his imagination completely.

"I want a train. My own train."

His parents laughed aloud, "*Bachela*, it is big, it is huge, one person cannot have a train. See, many people ride on it."

"No, no, I want a train. Please tell Gayla Lama or Chachey Limbu to do some magic. I know they can bring a train for me."

Seeing the child's interest, Gayla Lama, invited Chime Rinchen, a creative craftsman who was an expert in turning waste, discarded items into toys for children.

Rinchen accepted the challenge put to him. He collected the discarded juice cans, wires, rods and rubber bands. He watched many videos on You-tube to understand the working of railway engines.

His effort finally paid off. The play train ran chugging along on the table.

Inspired, Rinchen picked up thrown away chairs and pieces of metal to cut rails, using bicycle rims as wheels. In a year, he had a toy train running in the monastery playground, named GAUNCHA EXPRESS.

A train had arrived in the mountains of Gauncha.

The pictures went viral, getting likes for the creative artist Rinchen.

Chachey Limbu saw the video. He couldn't believe that his compatriot was doing such wonders.

For his part, he began to send DIY kits, to encourage children towards innovative ideas.

The children had enough on their hands during the vacation, the wonders of creation were their friends for life.

When bored with DIY, they would run and run the GAUNCHA EXPRESS, one day Telsang was the auto-pilot, the following day he was the guard, another day a simple passenger. His friends would also take turns to be the guard, signalman, passenger, auto-pilot, a porter or Station Master.

The youngest ones ubable to manage the role play, would place their tiny palms on another child and run about imitating the train sound "Kuuuuu, chuk, chuk, chuk... Kuu."

Gayla Lama would look out of his window, smiling and wondering if the children would permit him to join their train game.

Do you think they would?

21

The Crash

I, Romeela, sat in the A C coach of the Capital Metro, returning from my College of Pedagogical Training at Swatinakshatra to my PG at Rannbazzar, accompanied by Durga.

"Too hot, switch on the AC turn to 10."

"Damm, it's not functioning, exactly like my brain, jammed during the exam, now the answers are floating in and out, like dead fish in a rotting pond."

"Let's move to the front, the A C and fan both are working there."

We pushed, bumped, poked to reach the cool area. Cool compared to the rear end of the coach.

Jayanti got off at her stop. We balanced ourselves on her seat, sharing space, hoping that someone would be kind enough to give a full seat.

We had risen early in the morning to study from two to six.

I took the '7:15' to reach the exam centre by 8:30, half an hour before the exam began.

Wrote the exam between 9 and Noon, boarded the train at 12:30. The early rise, exam, noontime and sweltering heat of May made us drowsy.

Perspiration rolled down, in spite of the fan and AC, our eyelids closed, while we held on to the base of the seat, swaying with the motion of the train. Dreaming of leaving the paper incomplete and missing the train, I was asking Bishaay to purchase a frozen Aloe Fruit for me. For a change, he obliged without any excuses, purchasing my favourite pineapple pastry and a large potato puff. As I bit the puff 'krunch', the entire carriage went crunch.

Screams surrounded me, someone stood on my upturned palm, while my hair was being pulled by a bag chain.

People were trying to get out, while others were trying to get in to help the bruised and injured.

I tried to get up, my knee collapsed

"Oo, I can't stand" I tried to use my free hand to hold the support bar and sit up.

"Here, give me your hand." I couldn't see the face, but I felt a strong, firm hand grip my palm and pull me up.

"Up, up, stand on the unfractured leg, hop, hop, let your weight fall on me." I was pulled out, almost dragged out. Flop, I fell on the overcrowded ground.

People crying in agony, luggage lying around, chaos and confusion. I adjusted my eyes to the sharp, bright noon light.

The coach ahead of us was derailed and had fallen to the side. The passengers were crying desperately for help.

The approaching sirens of the police cans, ambulances and a train on the next track created a lot of noise.

"The train crashed into a wrongly parked goods train."

"The track had been tampered with, an iron bar dug it out."

"The heat caused the engine to burst."

"At least thirty people dead, a hundred injured."

"We need more ambulances immediately."

"Here, have this water." I felt a cold piece of plastic being handed to me. It had been uncapped, I took a gulp and splashed some of the water on my face.

"Lie down, we will lift you onto a stretcher. Do you have a mobile? Give us a contact number."

I fazed out.

"Please, please, give us your name and a number, you are fine, not to worry." I found myself on a hospital bed, with a nurse dressed in pink talking to me.

"975****149 or 58******80"

"Thank you, who will respond?"

"Papa, Asgar Raahat

or Mumma, Raahat Asgar, Yes they accepted each other's name, I am their daughter, Asraa Ghat."

The nurse smiled and went away.

Where was my wallet? my mobile? My head was throbbing. The nurse returned with a cold juice and a packet of wafers.

"Hullo Asraa", a college volunteer, was there to look after me till a family member arrived.

"I am Tim, your assistant, let me know if you need anything. Not to worry, a fracture, six weeks of plaster."

Two days later, my parents were ready to take me home, staying in the PG was not possible and the attending doctors had permitted travel.

"How will we go?"

"By train."

I began to scream and shout involuntarily.

"No, no, no train, never, it will crash."

The counsellor along with my parents did their best to explain things logically, trying to reassure me that everything would be normal.

I shivered, sobbed and curled up into a ball.

The trauma had left me devastated.

Finally, three ambulances from point to point were arranged to take me home.

The effect of the train sound gives me the jitters, though I have re-learnt to board a train with my fingers, toes crossed.

My confidence crashed and fractured, my dreams of joining the teaching fraternity crashed and fractured, my future crashed and fractured, all because of a train crash!!

*****